Merry
CHRISTMAS

This Books Belongs To

....

....

....

....

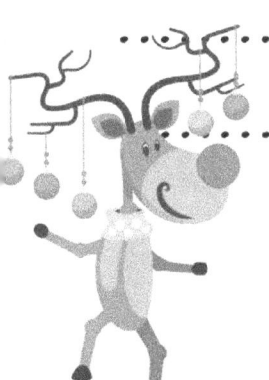

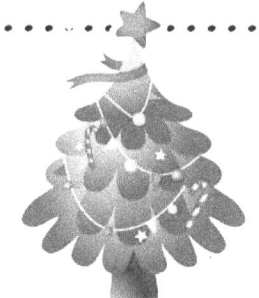

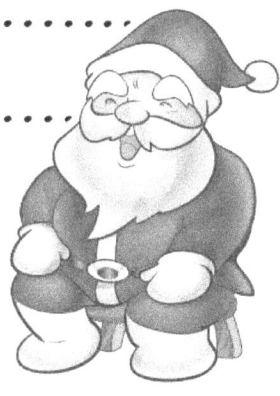

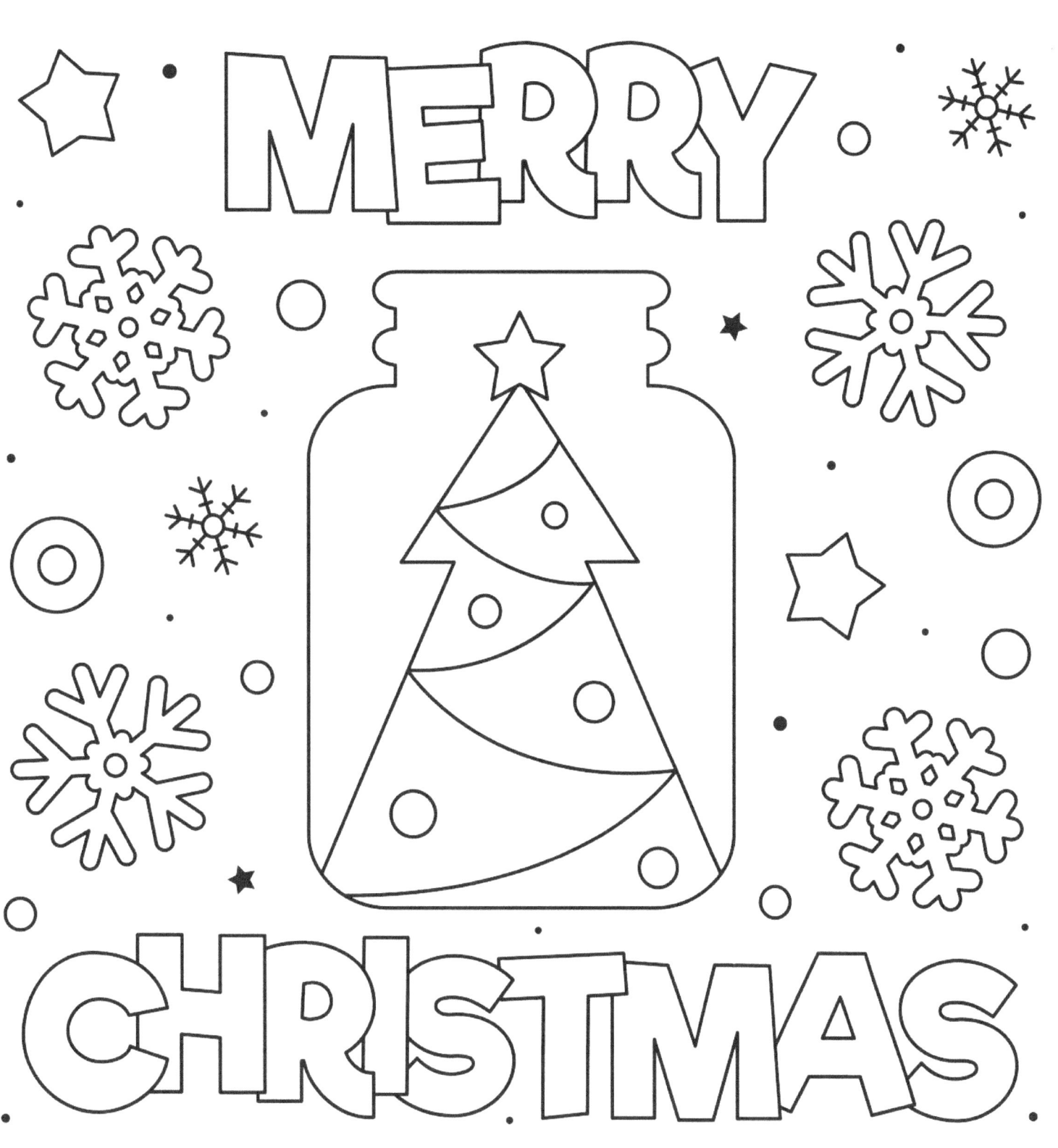

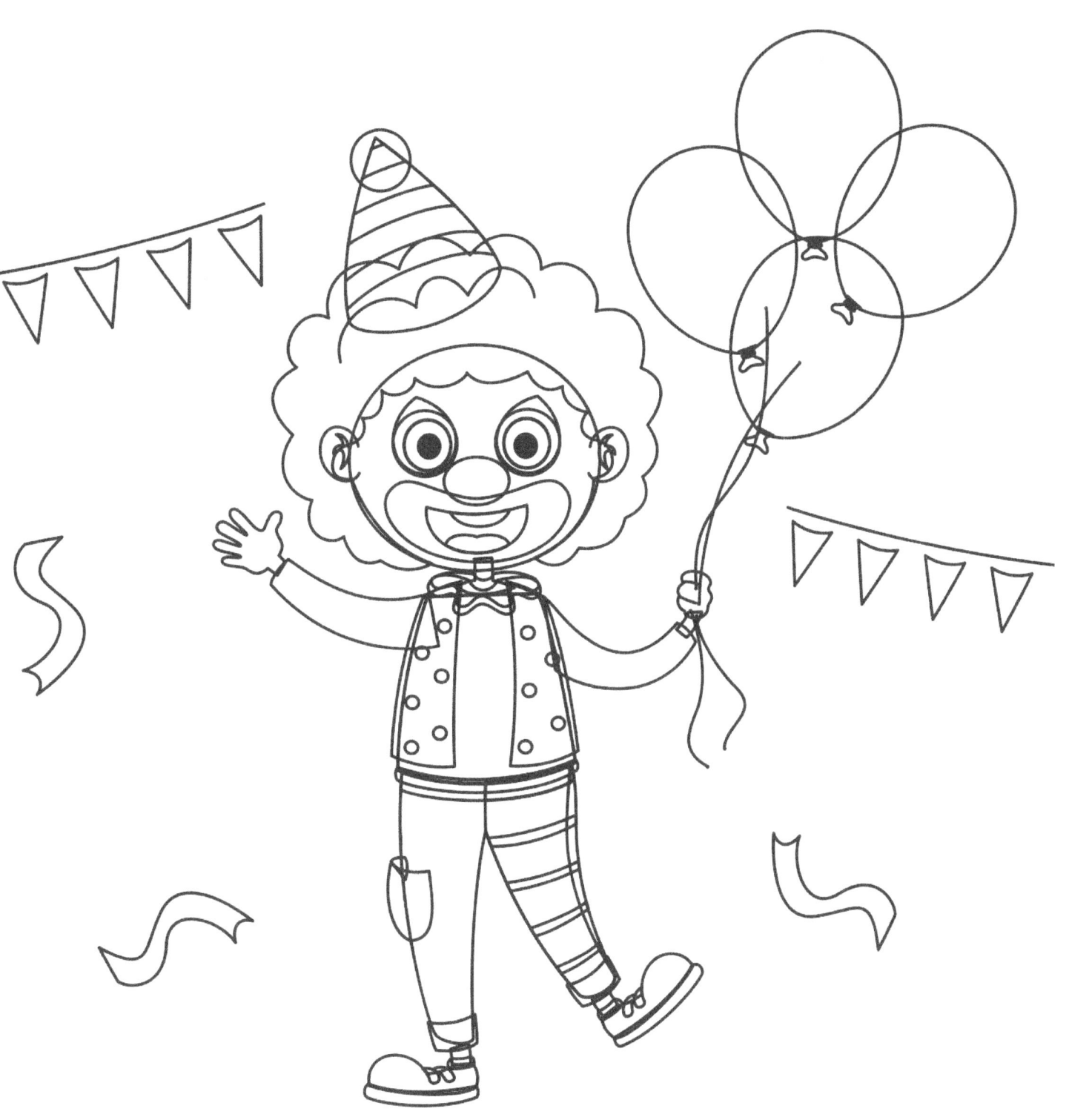

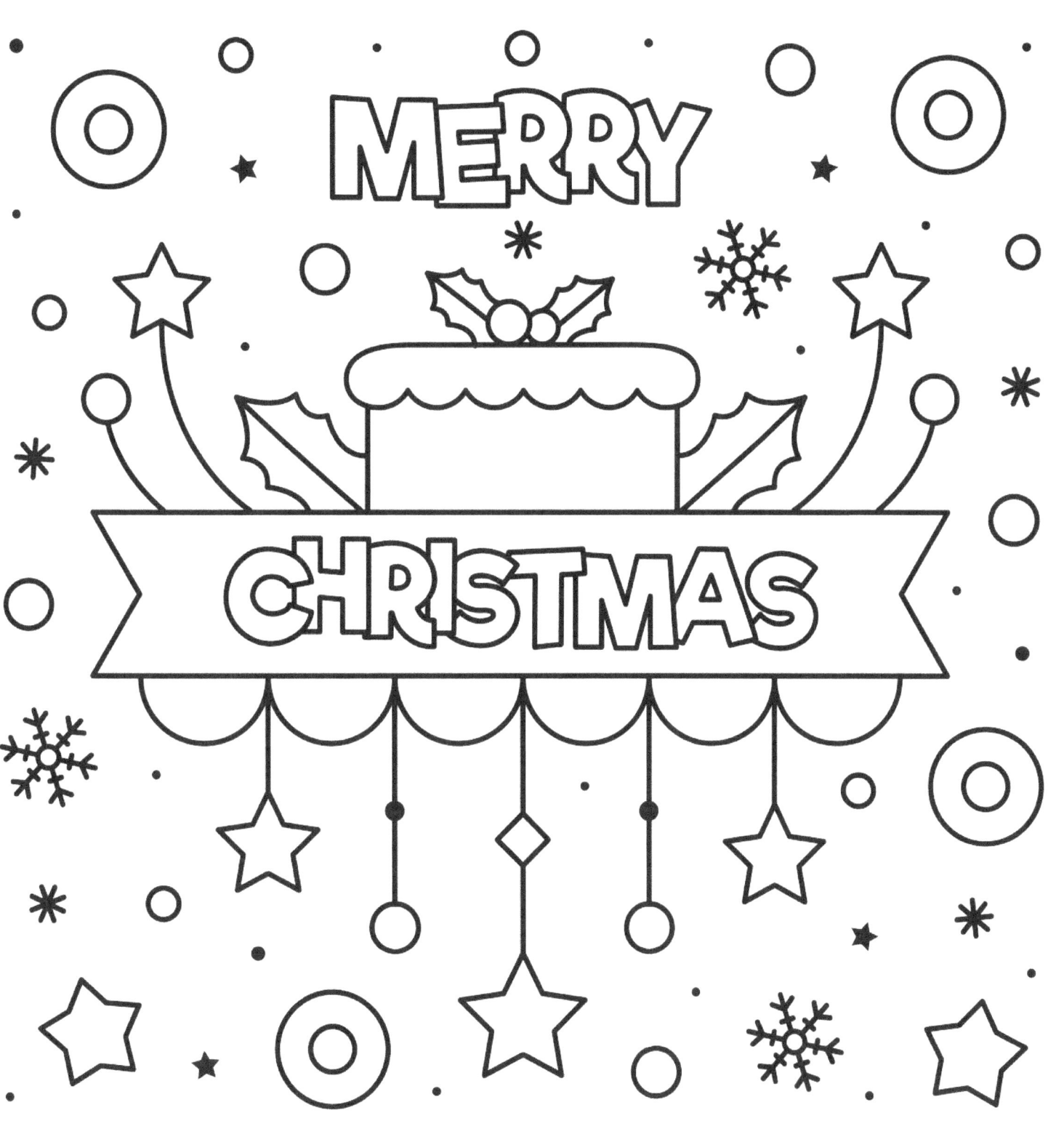

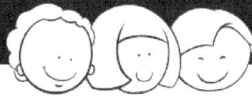

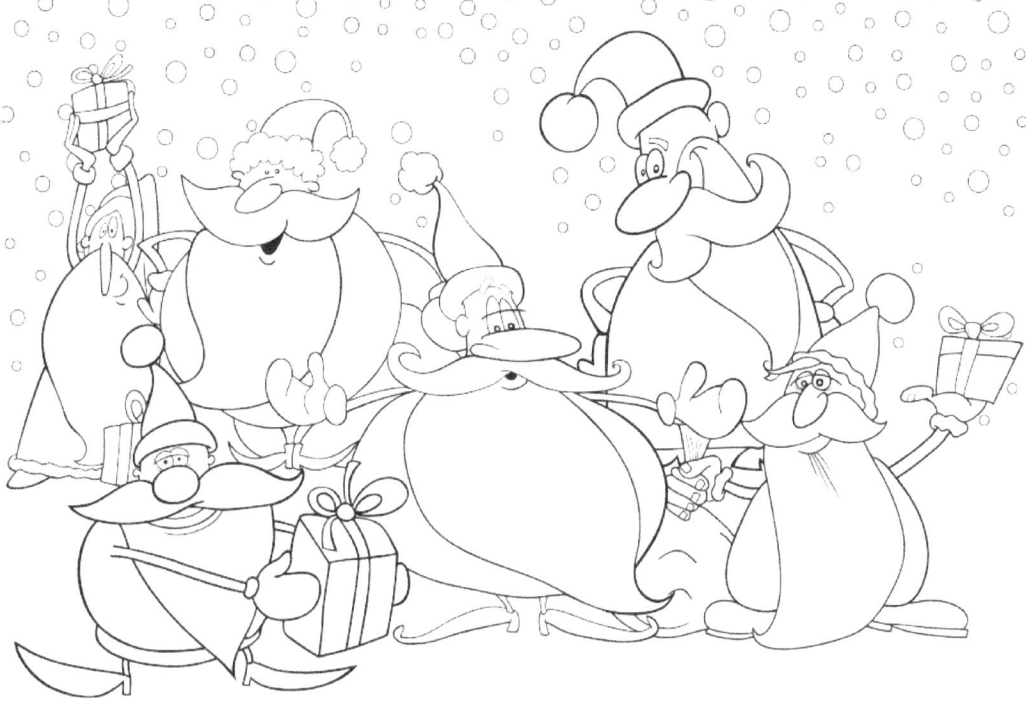

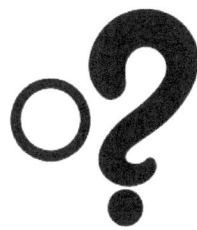

FIND
7
DIFFERENCES

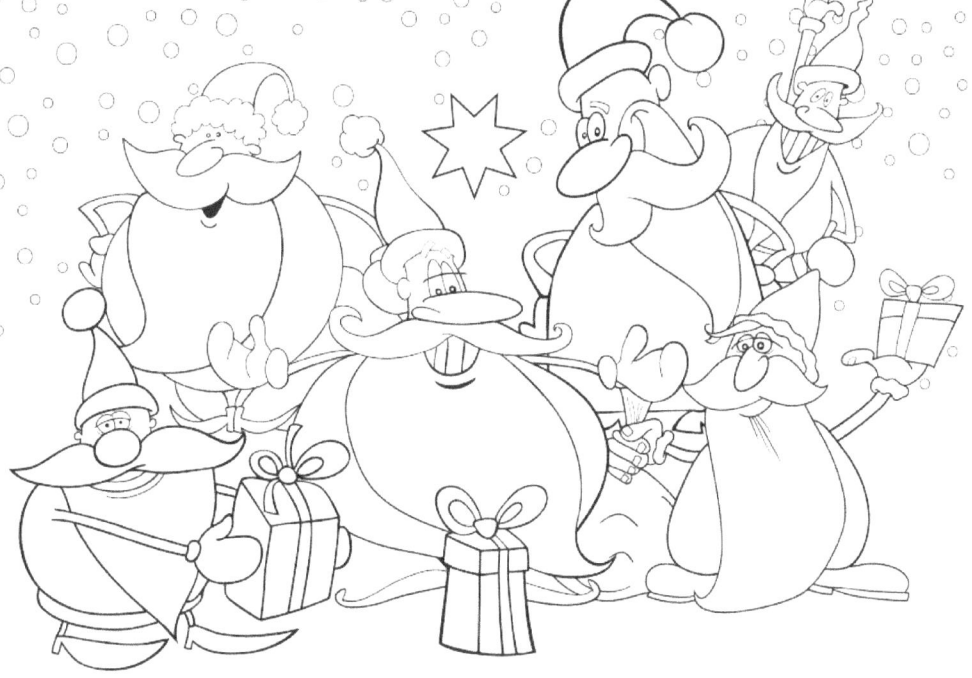

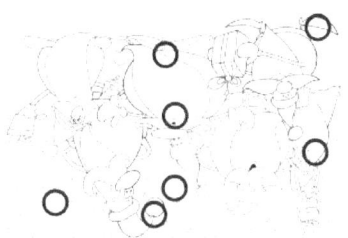

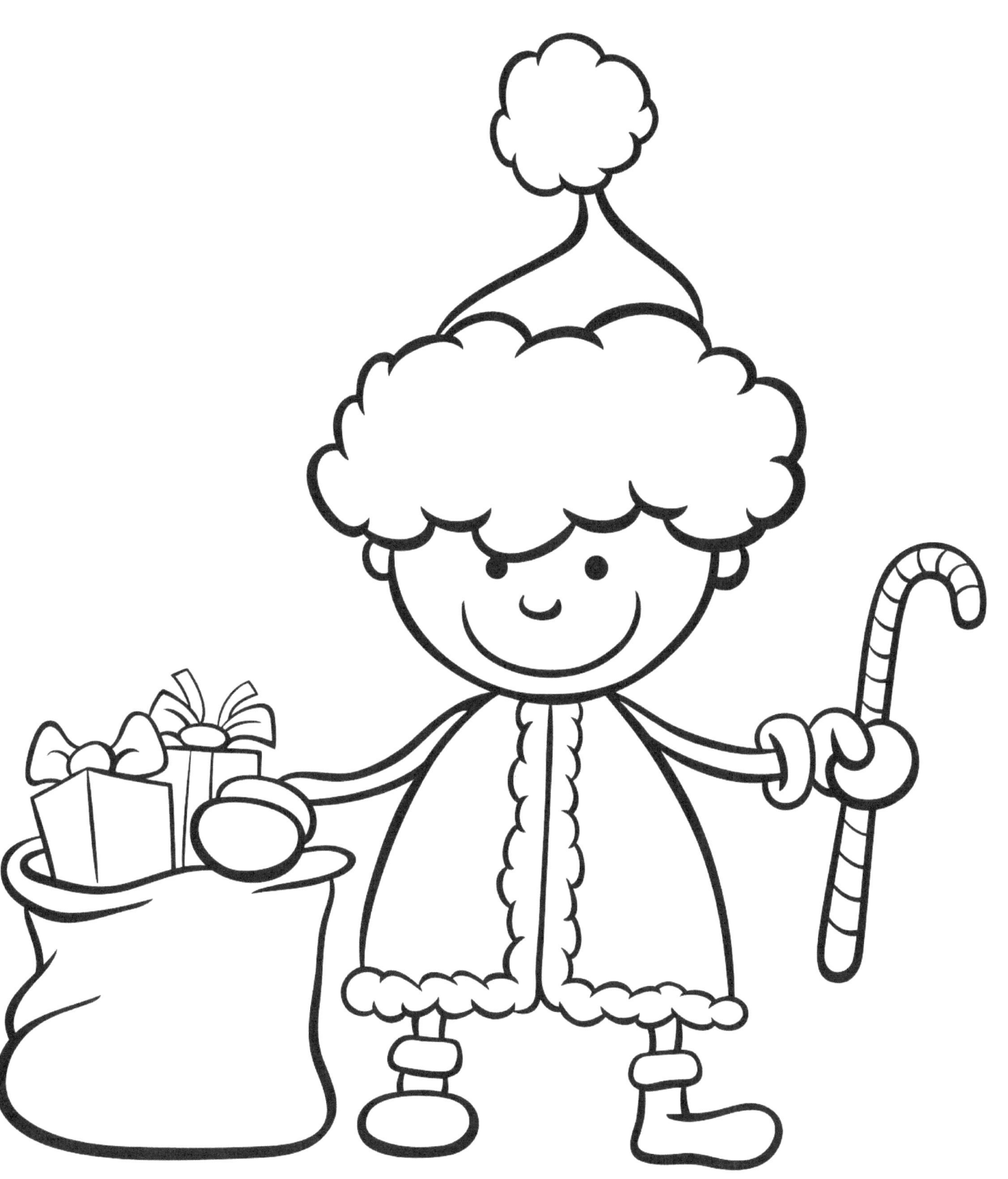

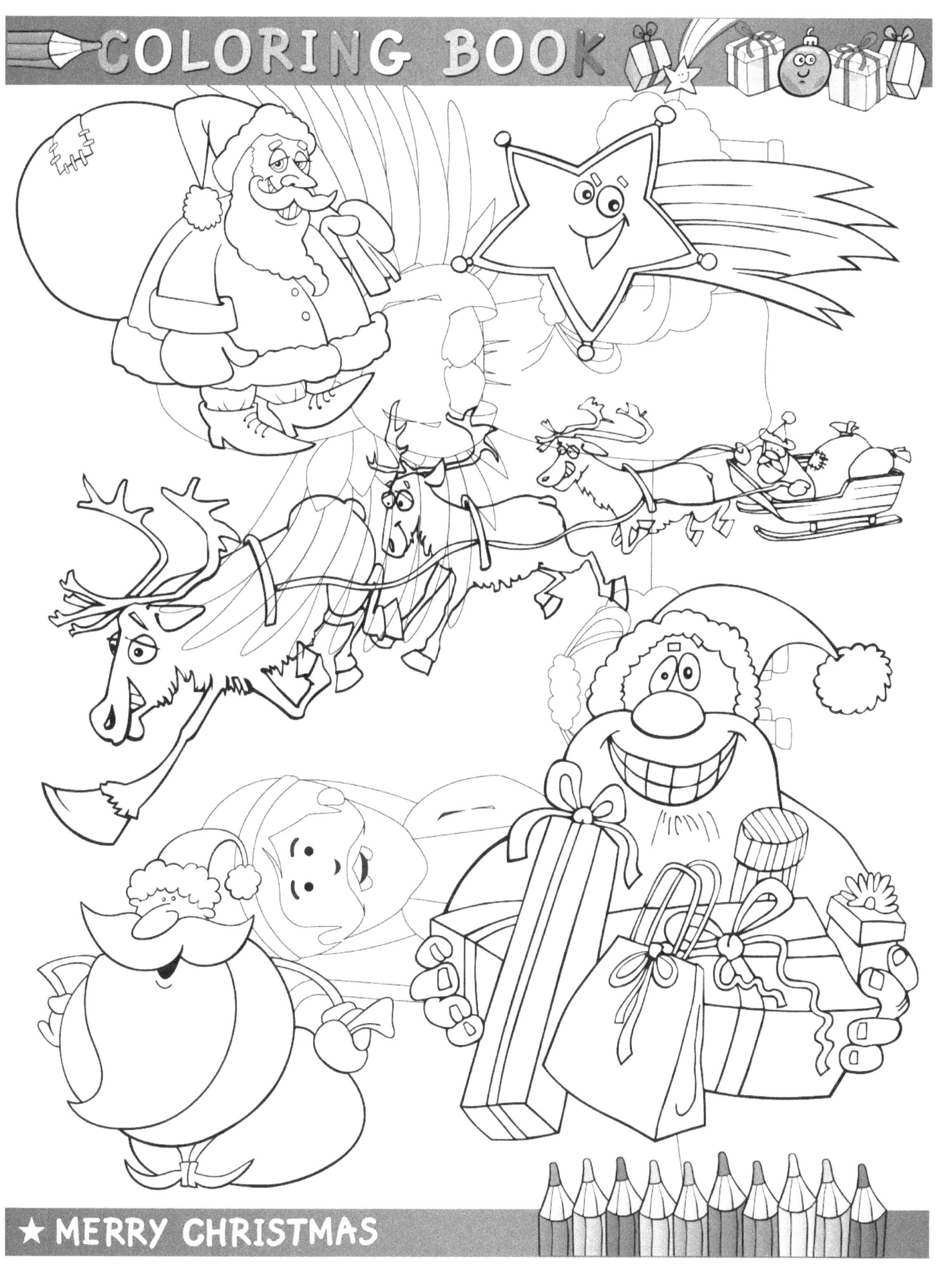

COLORING BOOK

★ MERRY CHRISTMAS

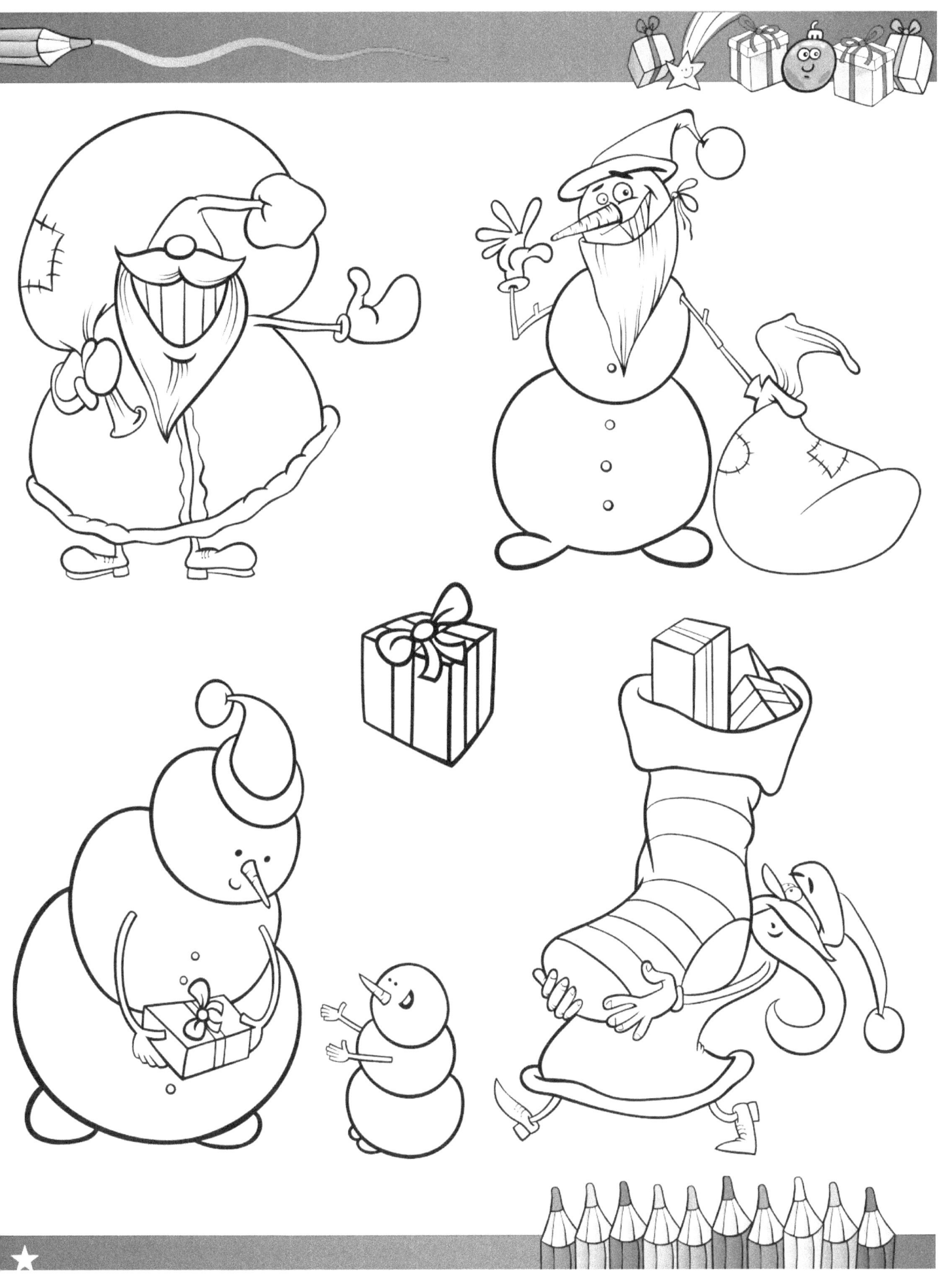

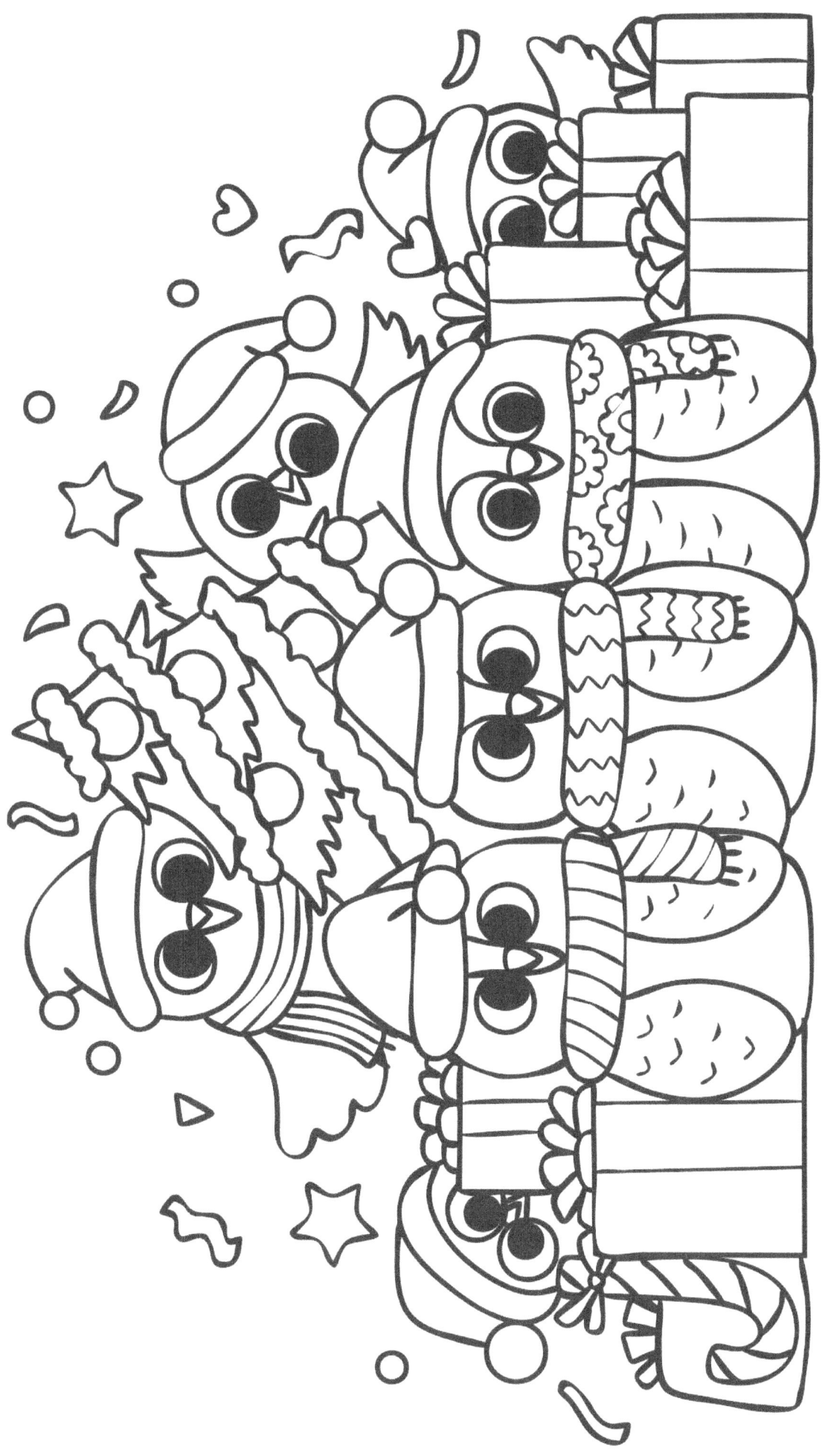

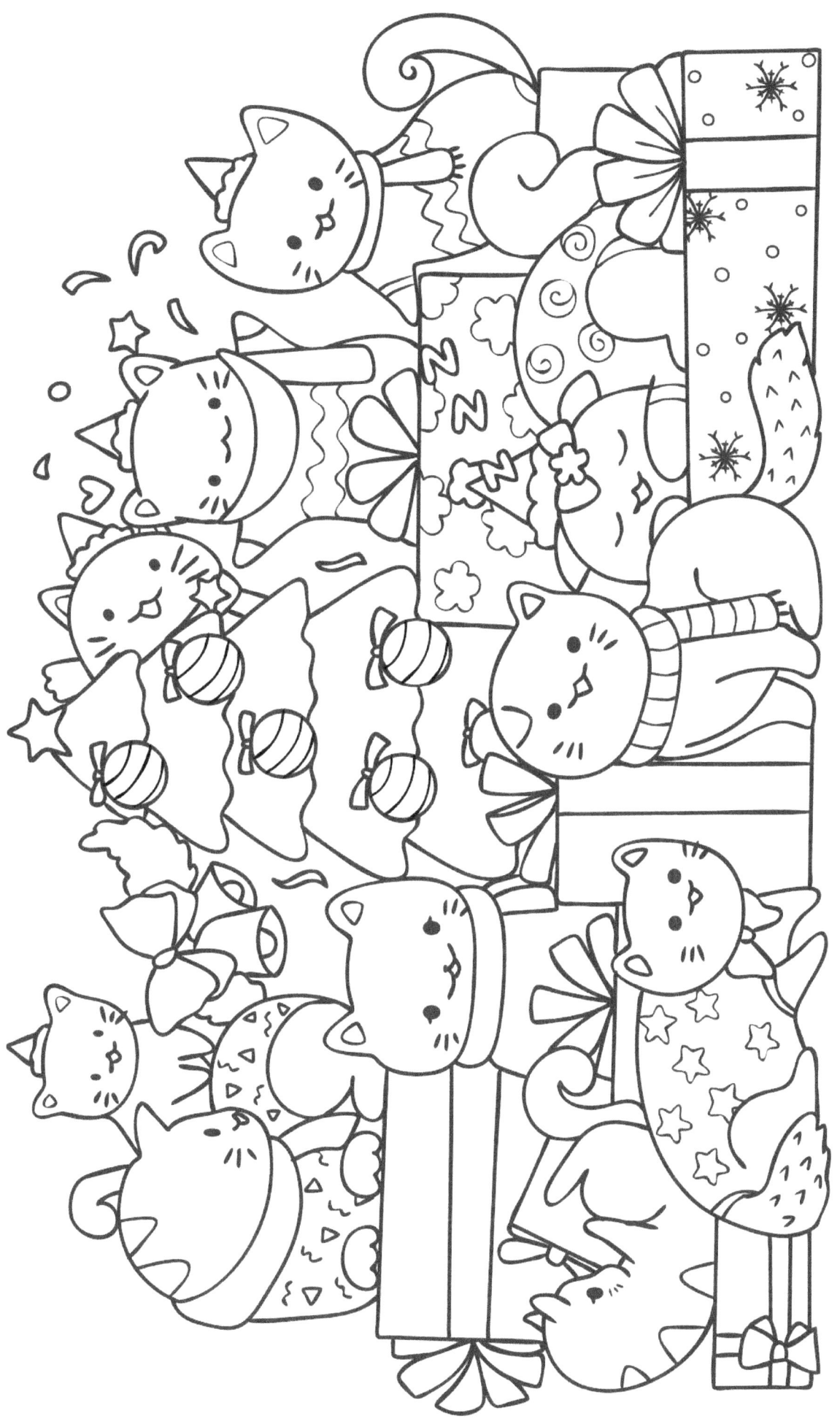

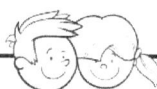

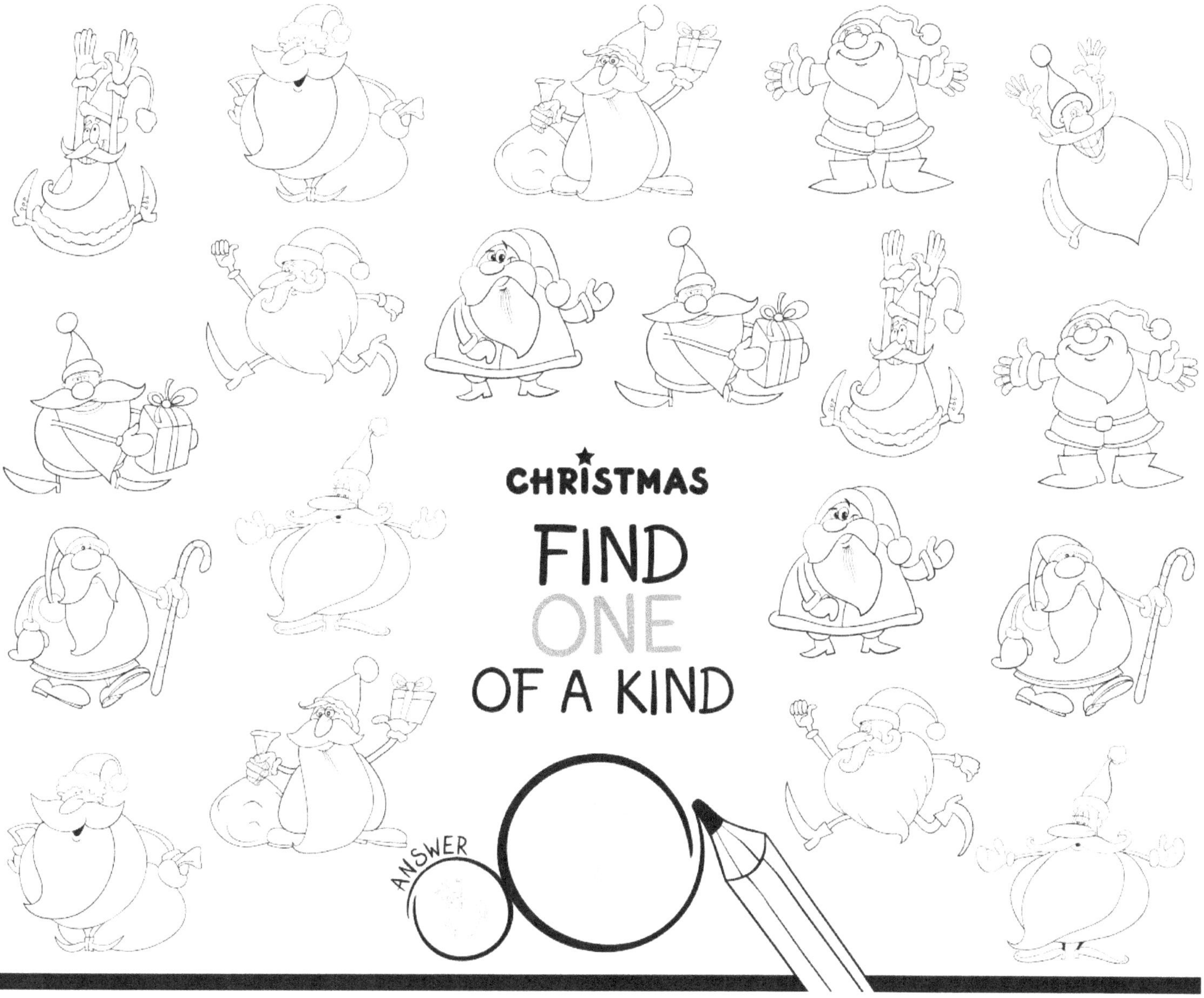

CHRISTMAS

FIND
ONE
OF A KIND

ANSWER

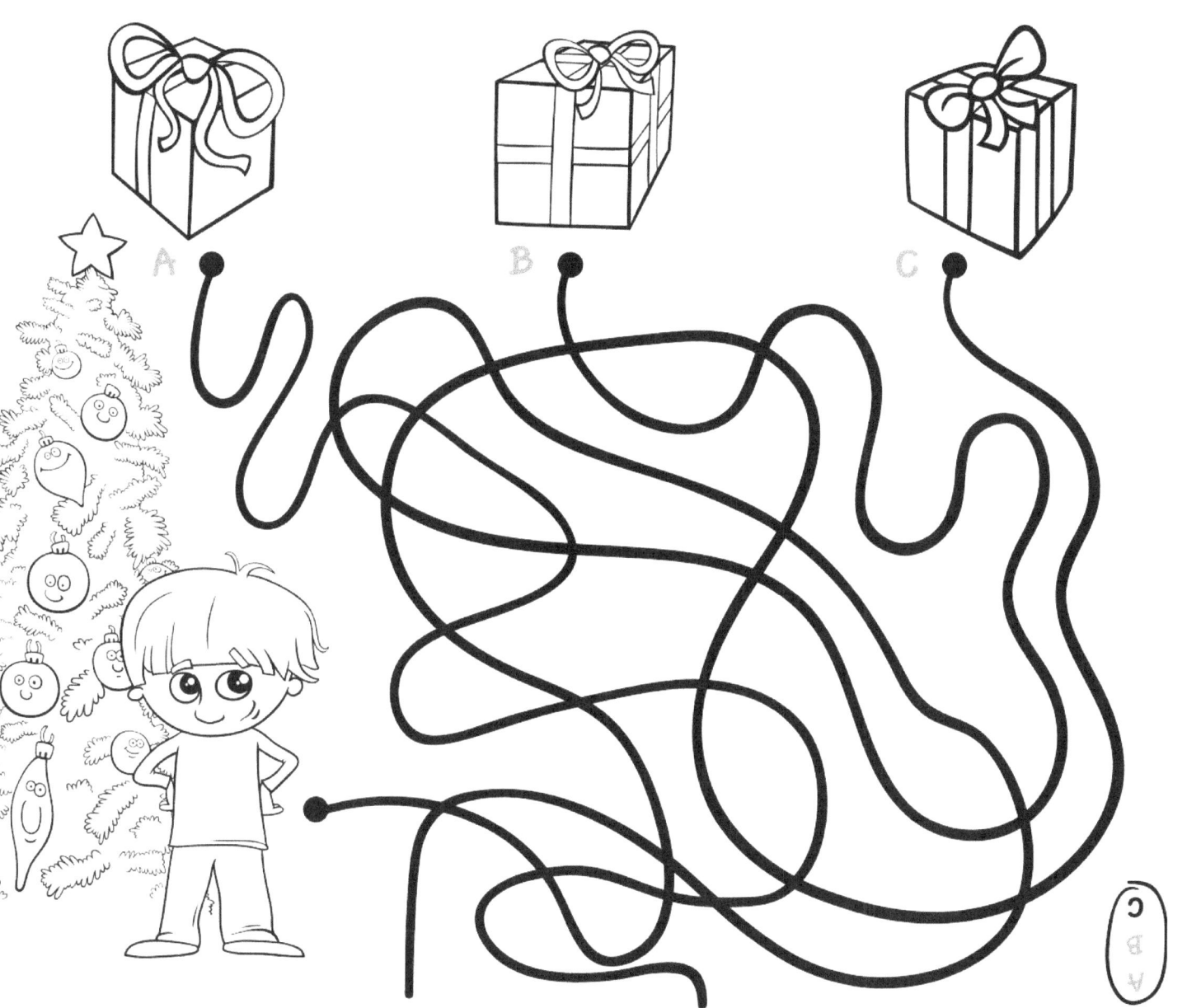

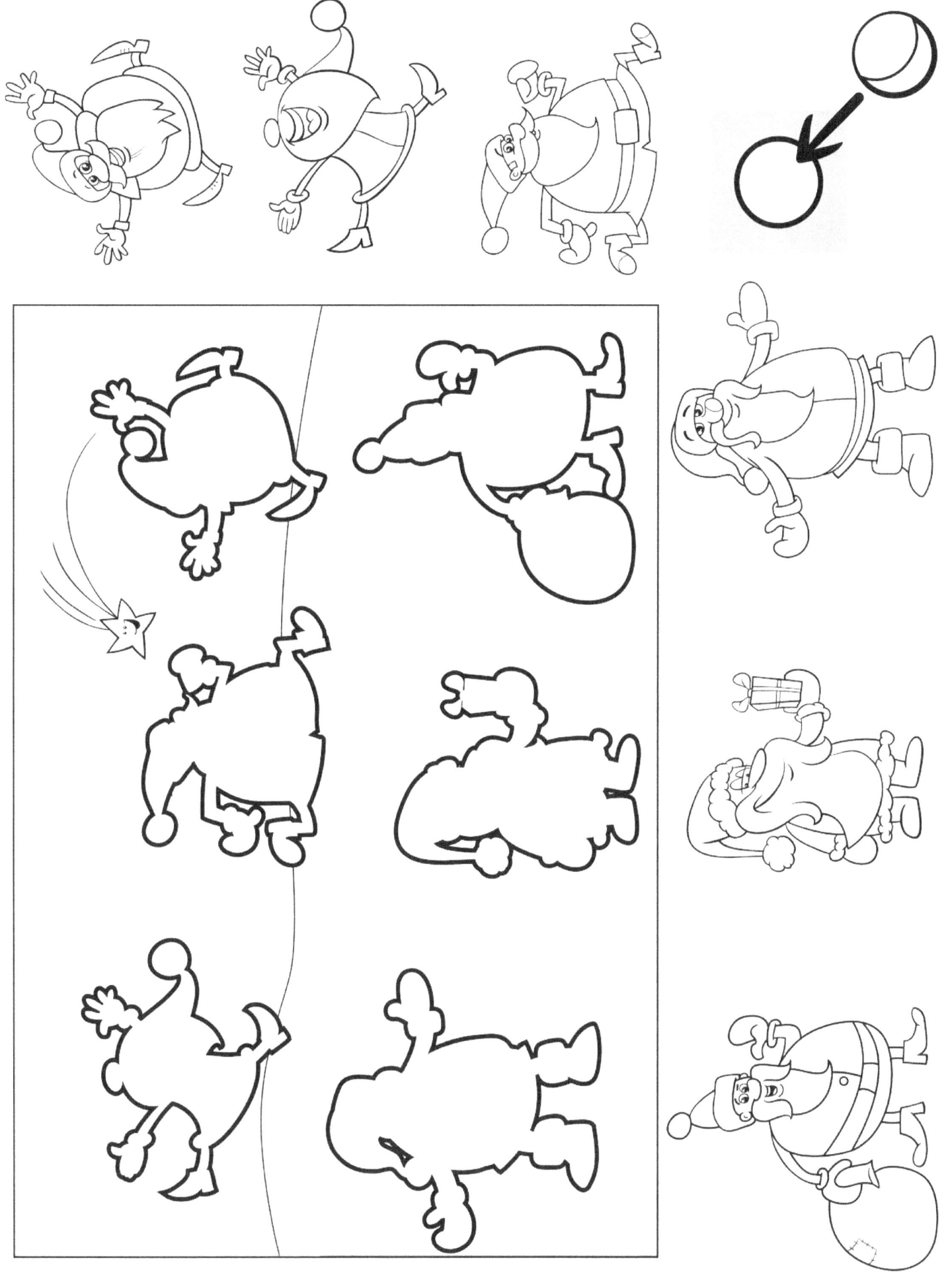

WHAT COMES NEXT?

ANSWER

1
2
3
4

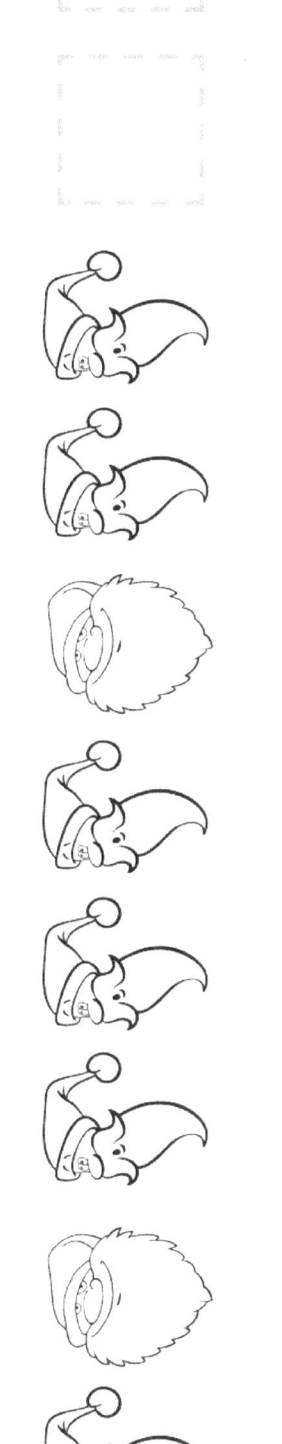
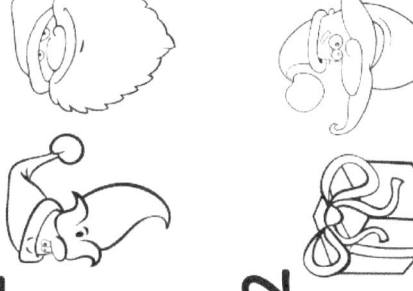
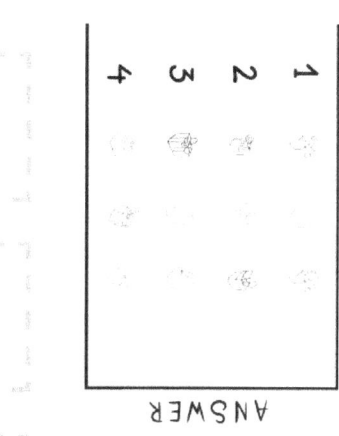

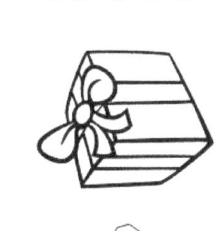
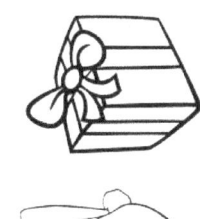
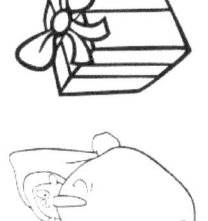
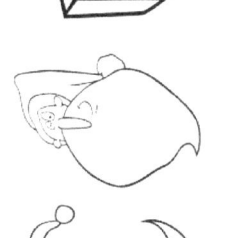
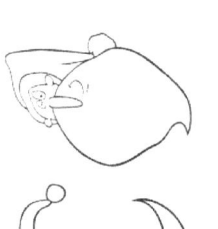
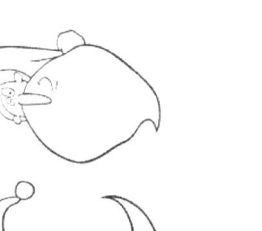
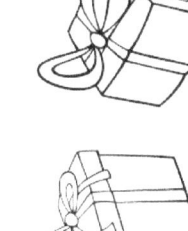
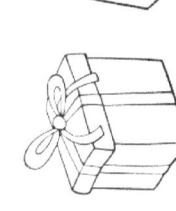
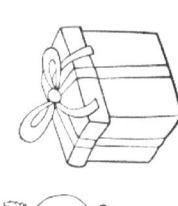
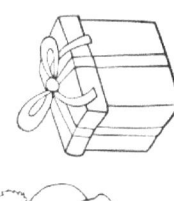
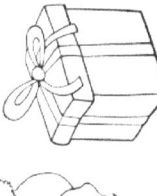
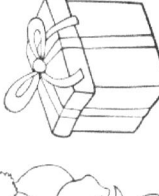
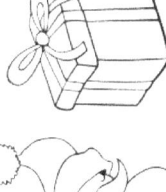
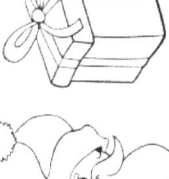
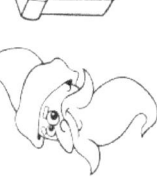
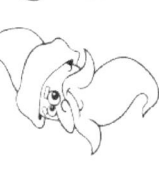
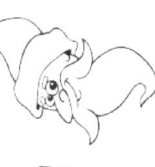
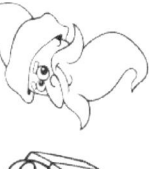
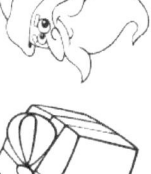
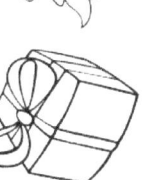
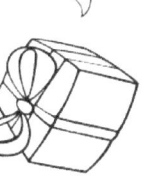
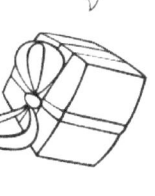
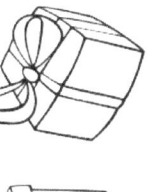
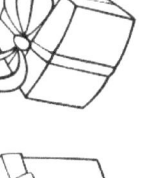
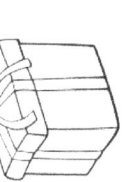
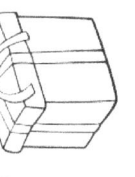
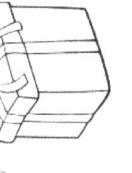
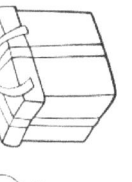
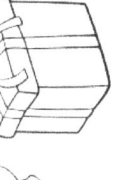
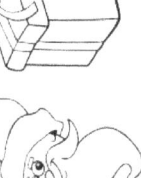
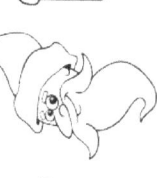
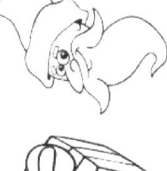
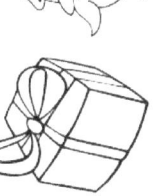
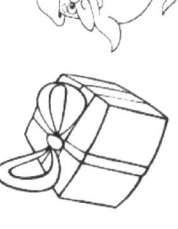
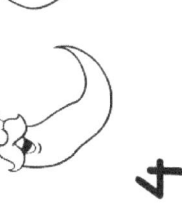

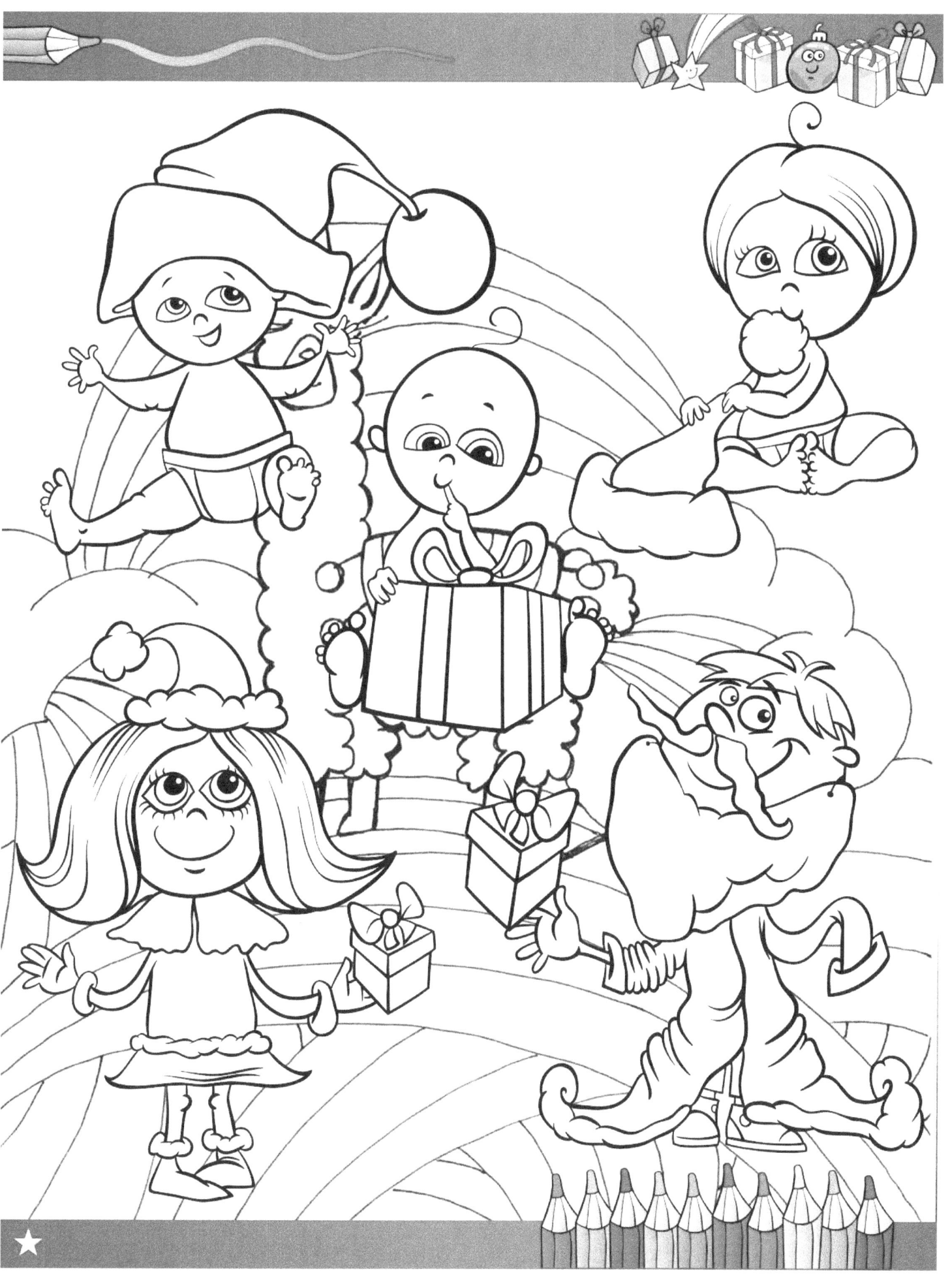

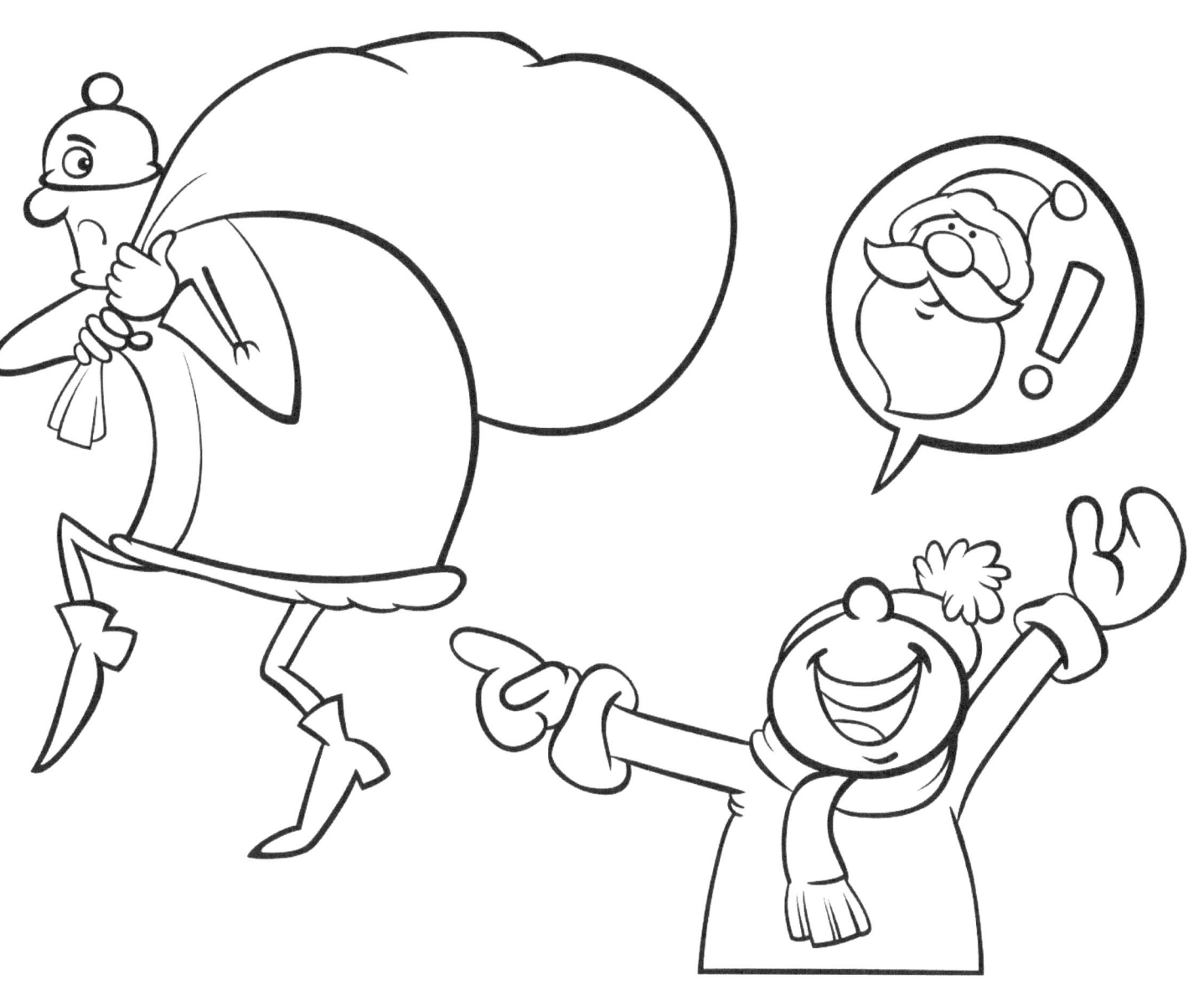

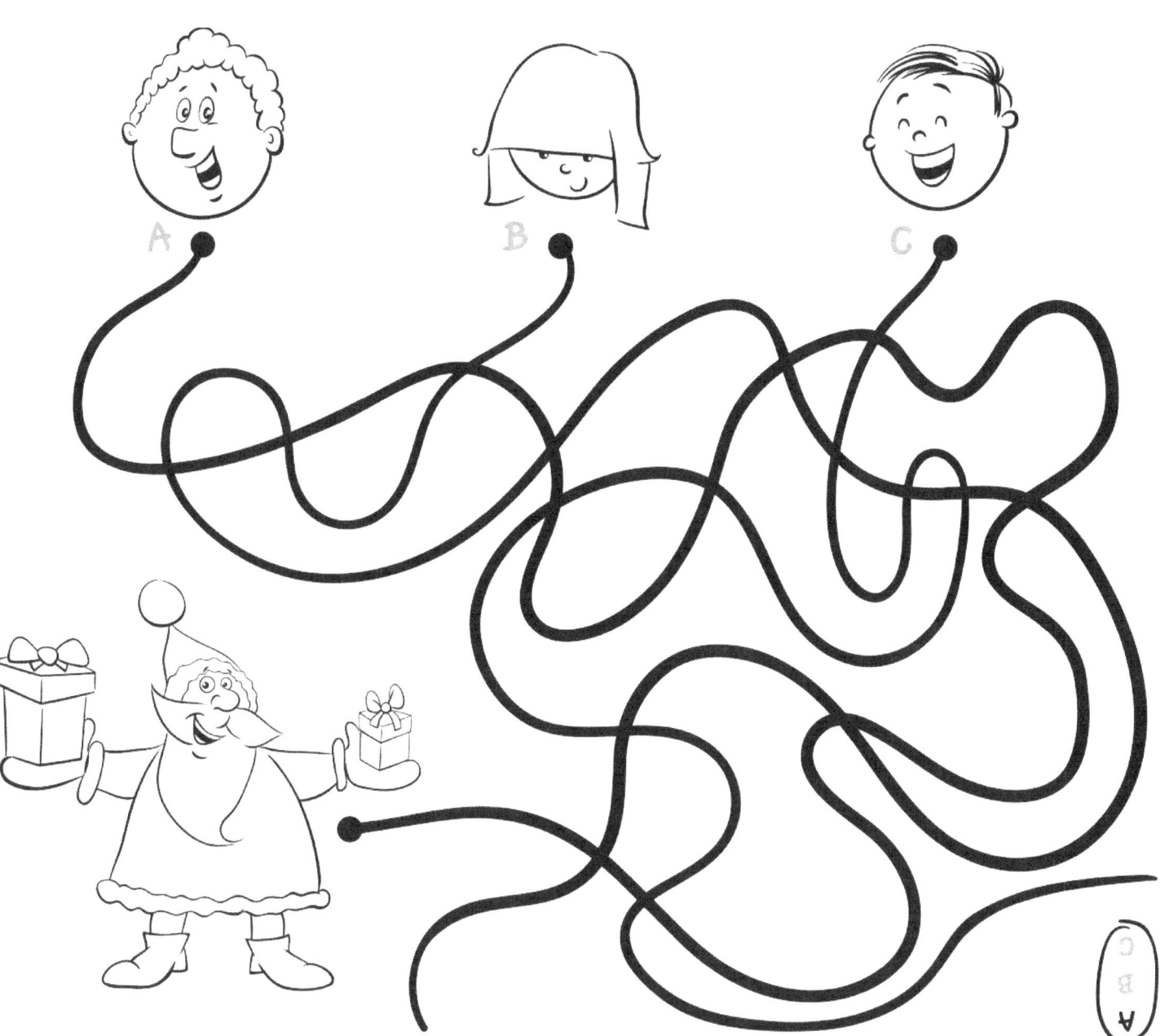

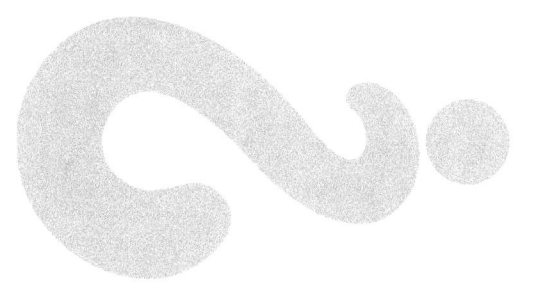
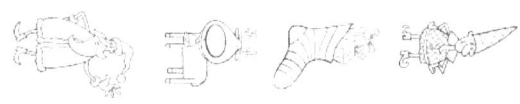
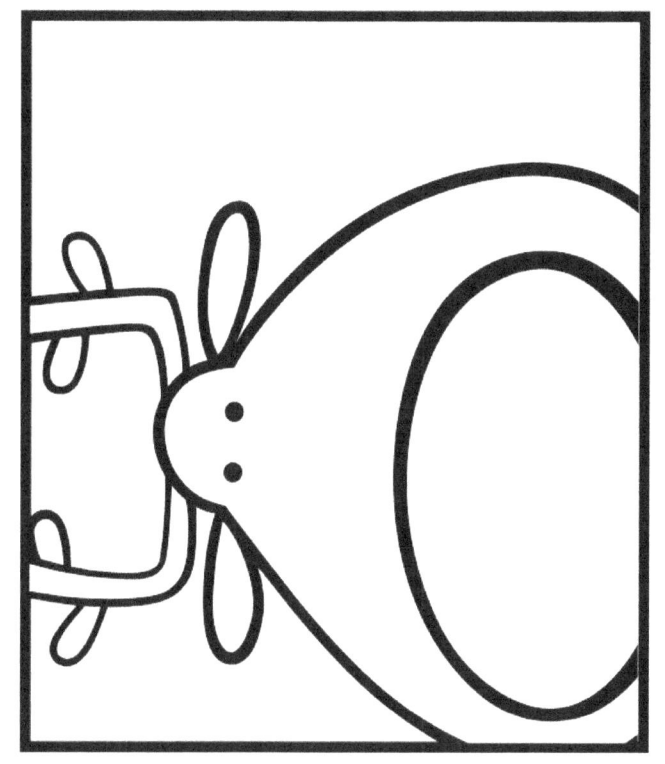
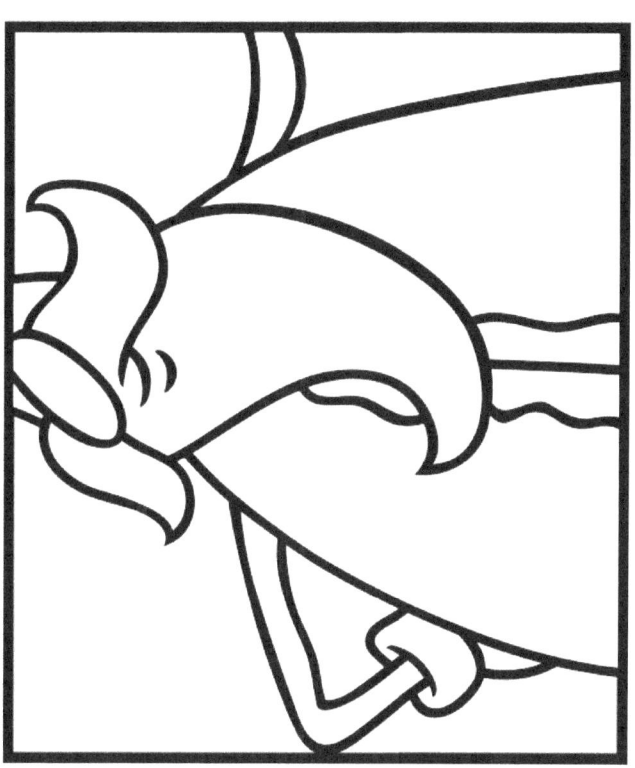
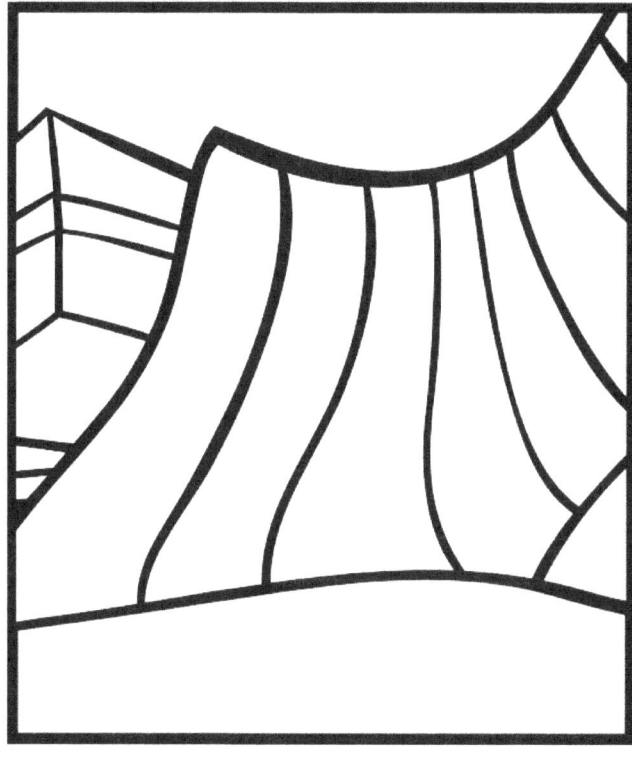
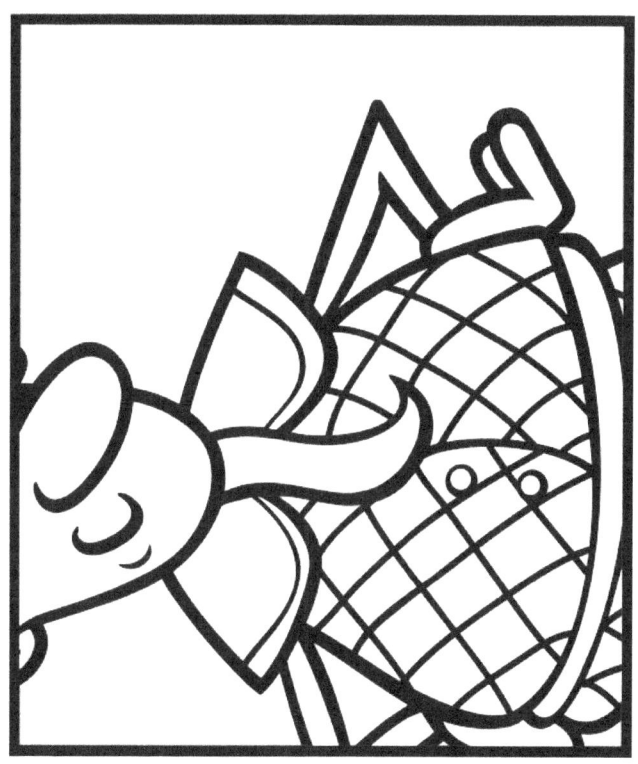

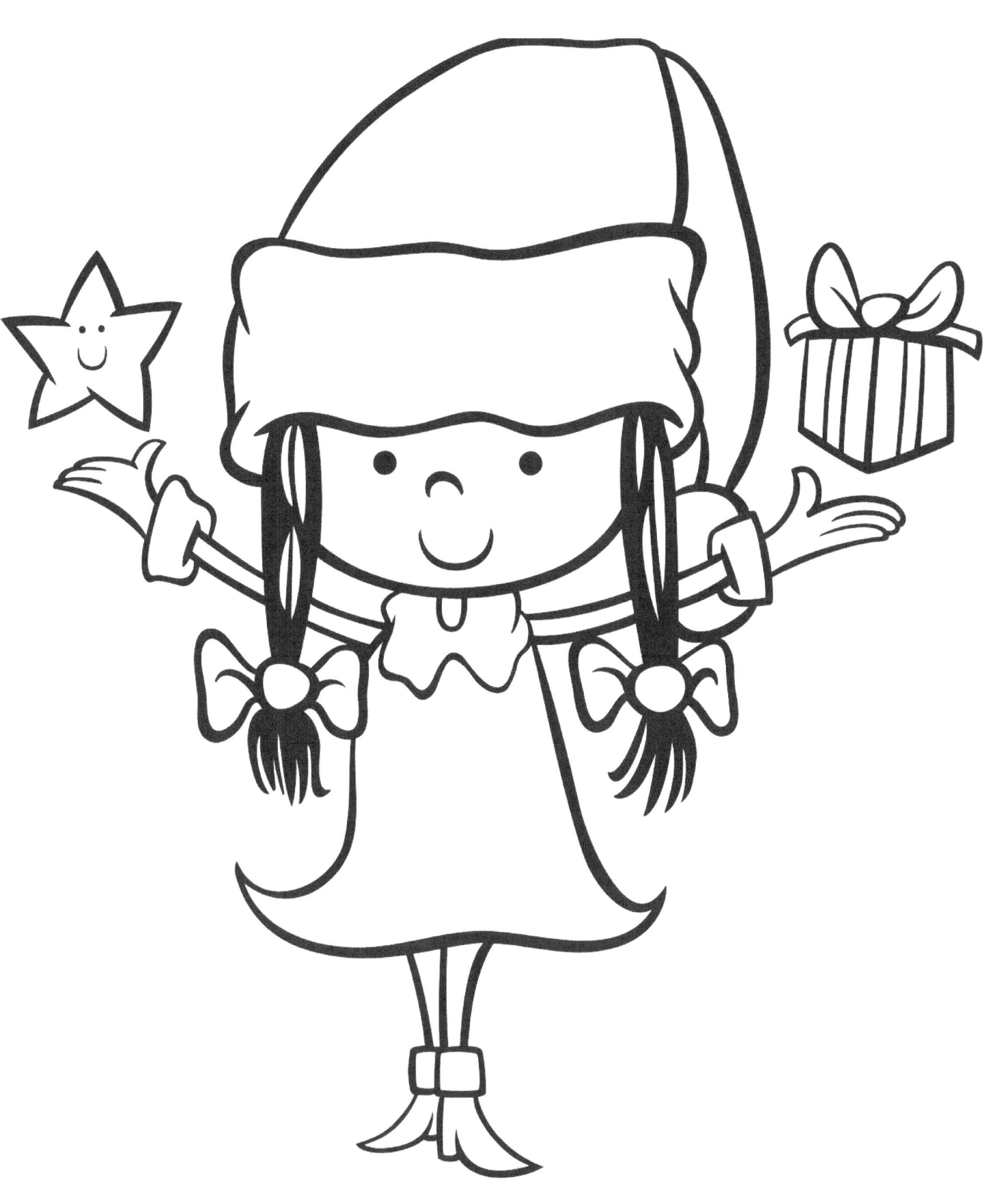

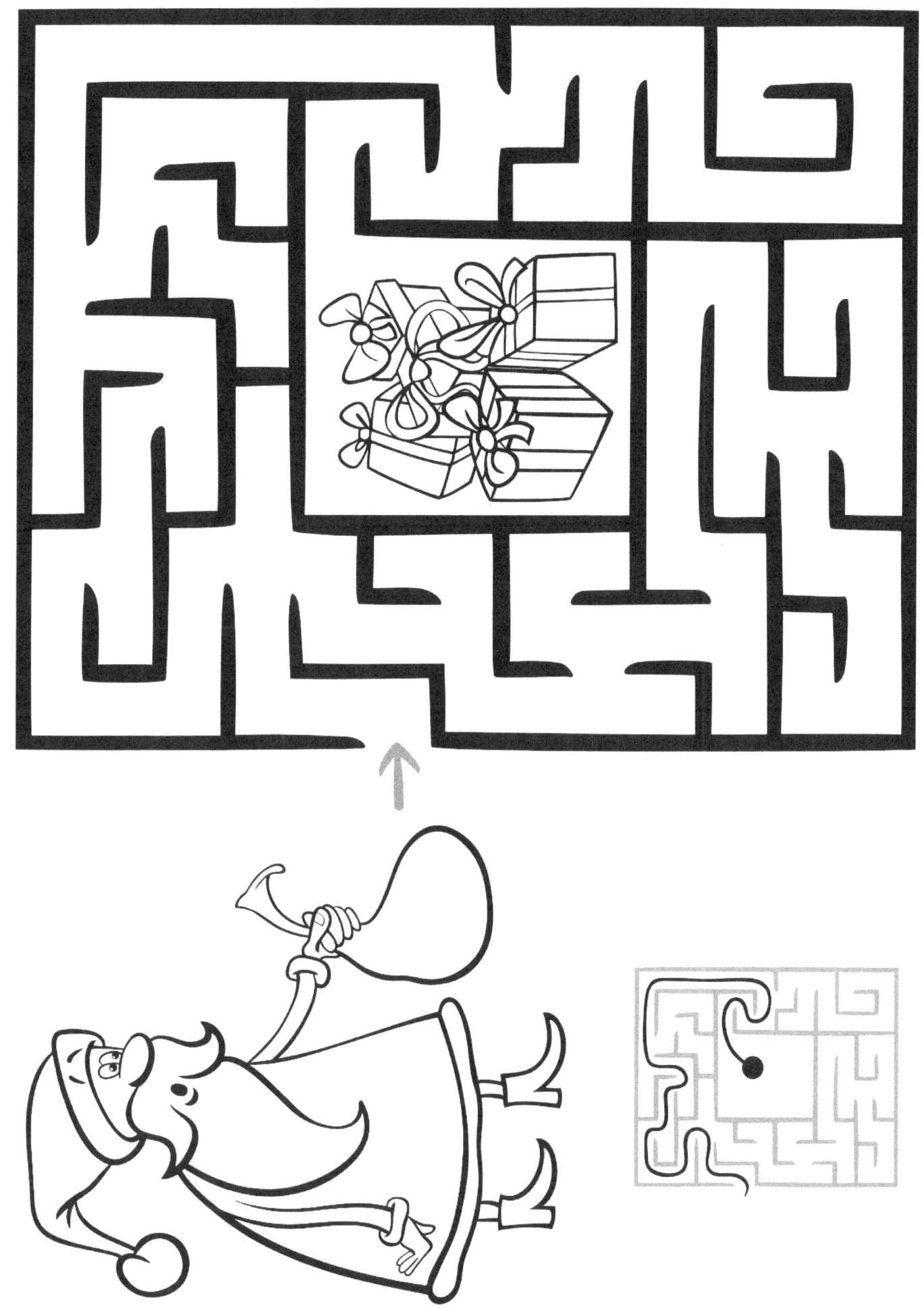

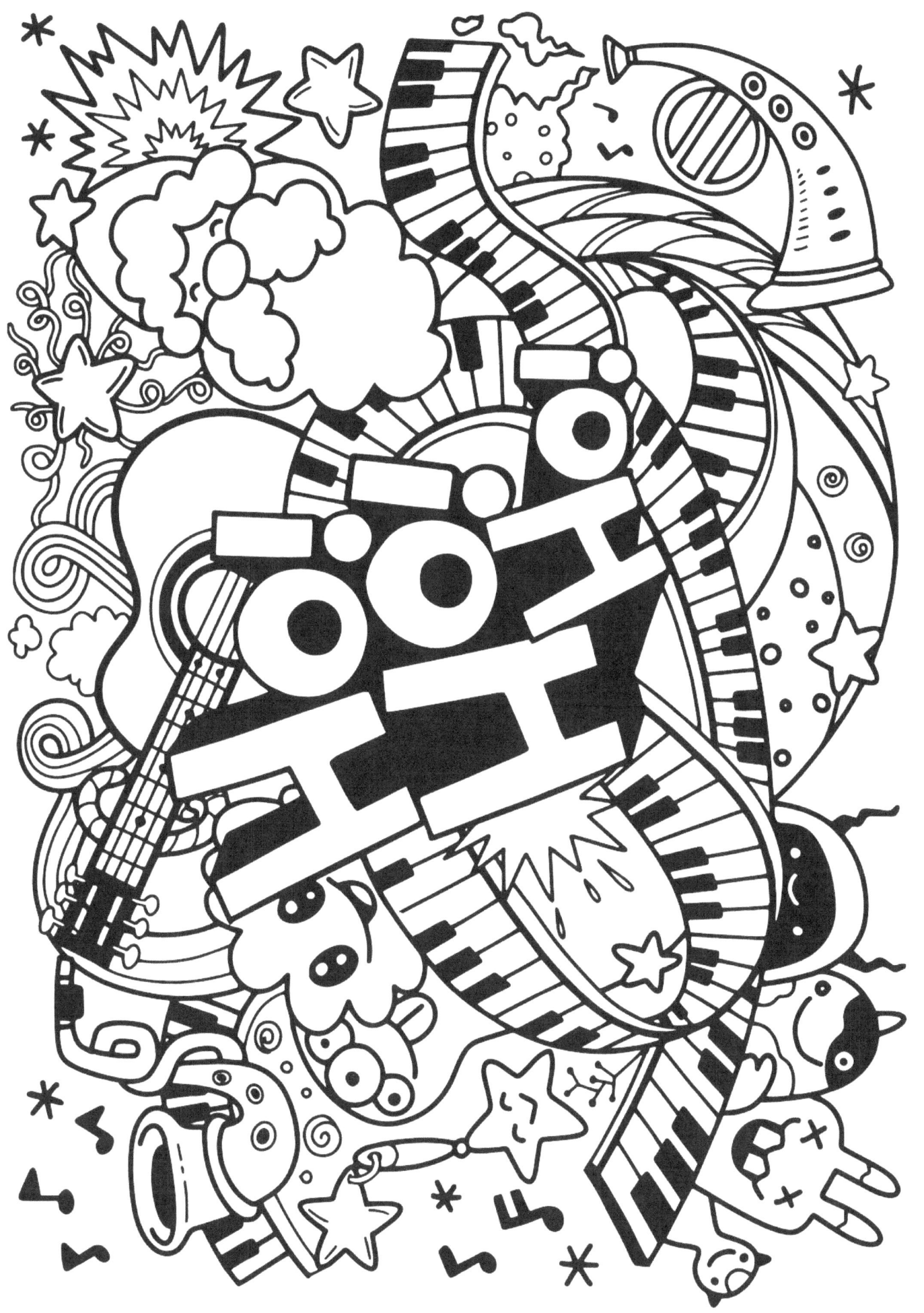

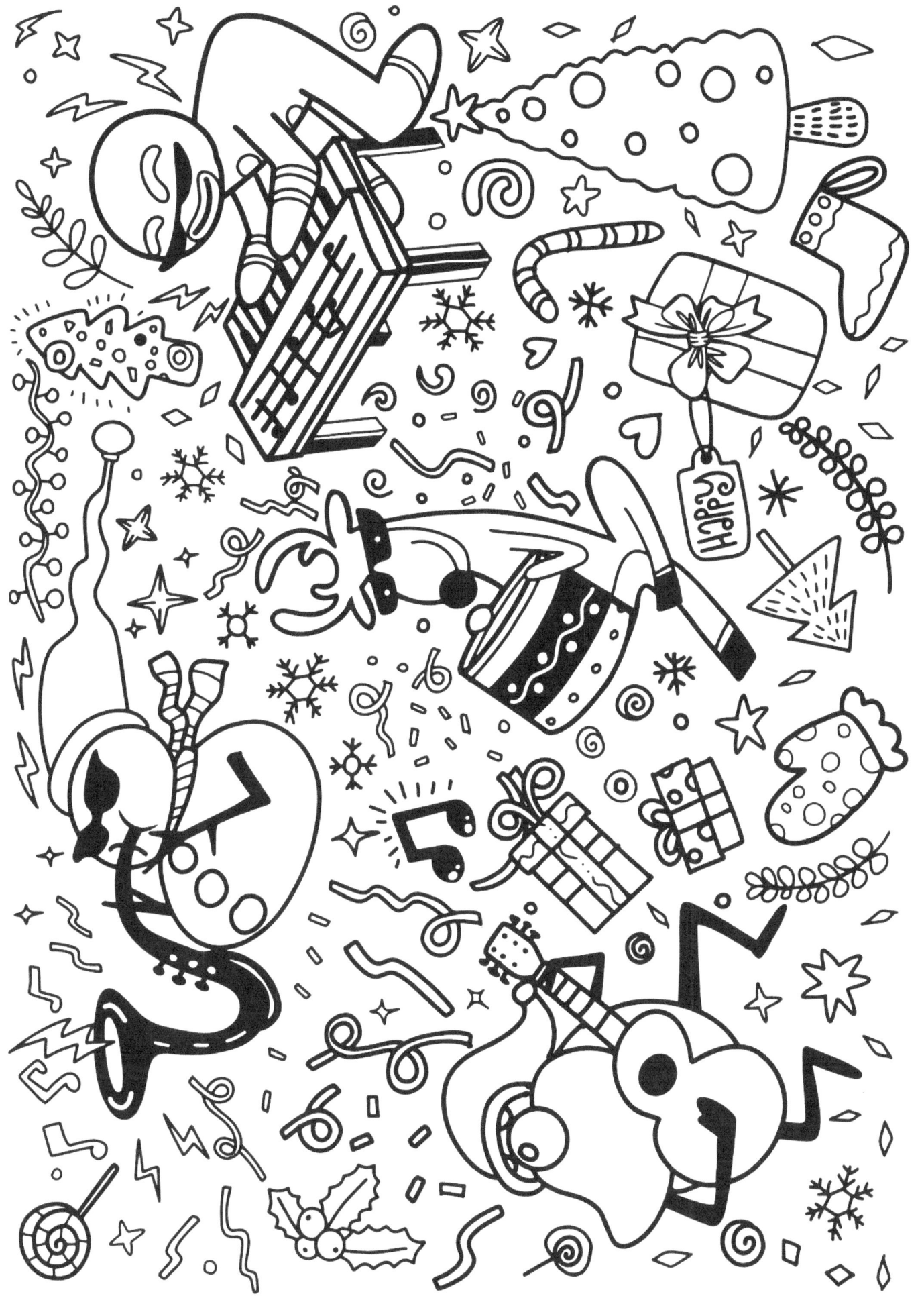

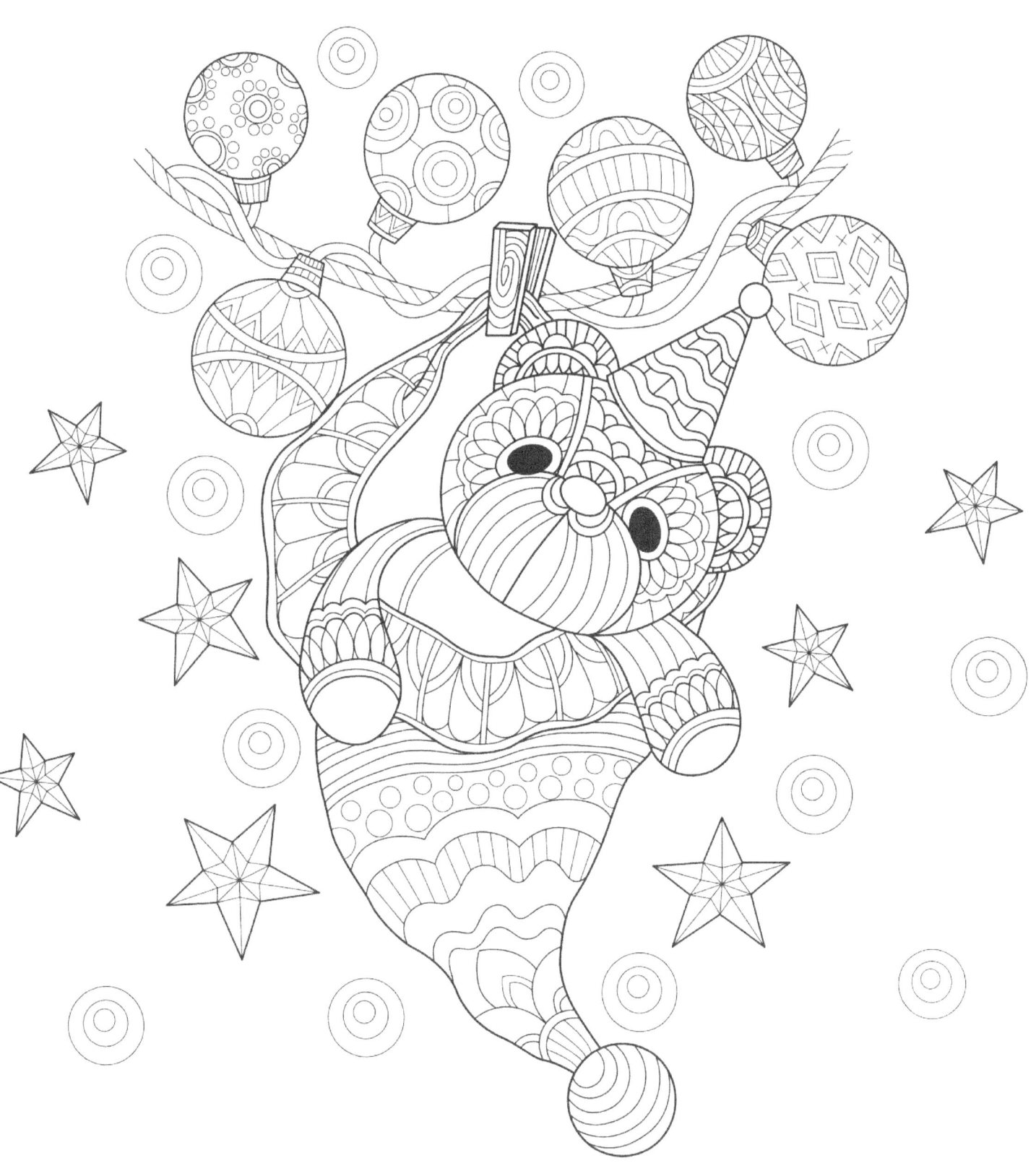

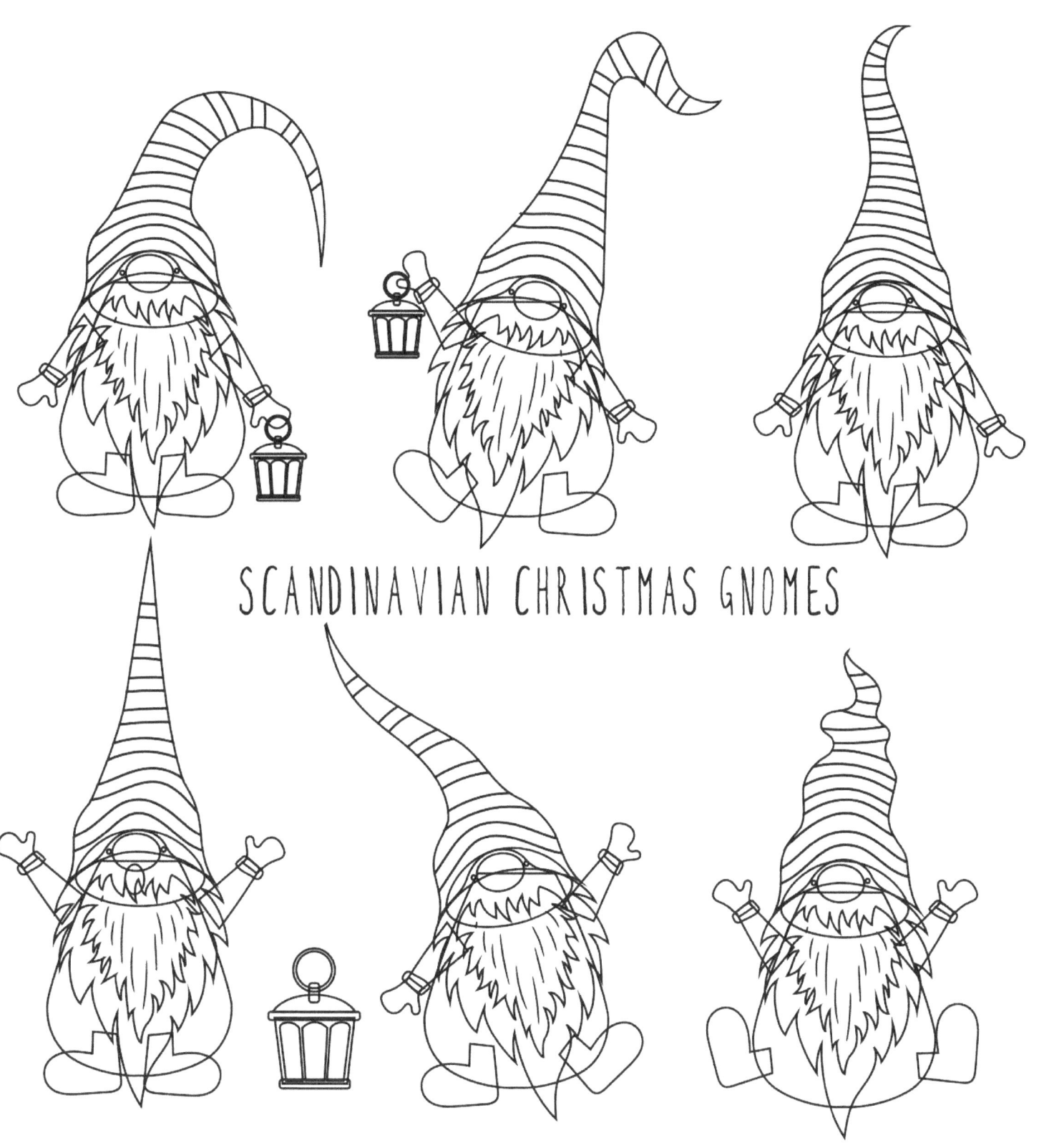

SCANDINAVIAN CHRISTMAS GNOMES

www.ingramcontent.com/pod-product-compliance
Lightning Source LLC
Chambersburg PA
CBHW081544220526
45467CB00010B/3318

9 7 8 1 7 0 5 4 9 0 9 5 2